In the Mind of Neural Networks

Getting Deeper Into AI

Table of Contents

Chapter 1. Introduction

Welcome to a riveting exploration that's guaranteed to pique your curiosity and enhance your understanding: "In the Mind of Neural Networks: Getting Deeper Into AI". This Special Report unravels the enigmatic world of artificial intelligence and neural networks, illuminated in a way that merges accessible description with substance, far removed from the often intimidating technical jargon. Regardless if you're an AI enthusiast or a neophyte embarking on an understanding of this groundbreaking technology, we confidently promise an engaging journey that's equally educational and intriguing. This report is not just about offering knowledge, it's about cultivating a deeper insight, about taking you on a tour into the mind of AI itself, and all in a language that feels comfortable and inviting to every reader. Prepare to break down barriers and immerse in the enthralling landscape of artificial intelligence like never before. Are you ready to dive in?

Chapter 2. Journey to the Center of AI: An Introduction

Brace yourself for a trip like no other—a descent into the digital neurons of the most revolutionary technology of our age: artificial intelligence (AI). The road ahead is a fascinating one, where you're not just understanding AI, but seeing it from a completely fresh perspective, as though you're journeying through its very mind.

AI, at its most fundamental level, is the endeavour to recreate human intelligence—emotions, comprehension, decision-making skills, and beyond—in a machine. Deep down, it's about unraveling the intricacies of our own cognitive processes and replicating them in an entirely new domain.

2.1. The Dawn of AI

Our journey begins with the genesis of AI. The concept may seem like 21st-century technology, but its roots date back to the dawn of human civilization itself. We've always strived to automate tasks and create tools that can mimic human behavior. The ancient Greeks had myths about robot-like beings, while in the medieval era, people designed self-operating machines called automata.

Our modern understanding of AI was born in the mid-20th century. Recognised as the "father of AI," Alan Turing, a British mathematician, raised the tantalizing question in his 1950 seminal paper, "Can machines think?" This paper laid the groundwork for a new field dedicated to answering Turing's question, which we now know as AI.

2.2. From Theory to Reality

The journey from Turing's ideas to real-world AI has been a winding road, marked by sporadic breakthroughs and enduring winters of slow progress. The first significant milestone came in the 1950s and 60s, with the emergence of symbolic AI or "good old-fashioned AI". Symbolic AI emphasized clear logical rules and precise calculations - the word 'robot', for instance, would be defined by a set of rules instead of patterns in data.

Although symbolic AI achieved some success, it was overshadowed by the advent of machine learning in the 1980s. Machine learning takes a fundamentally different approach—it lets algorithms learn on their own by recognizing patterns in data.

Fast forward to the 21st century, and we're in the midst of an AI explosion, fueled by a variant called deep learning and enriched by our collective advancements in computing power and data generation capabilities.

2.3. Decoding Neural Networks

Deep learning's rise has been underpinned by an innovation that forms the bedrock of modern AI: neural networks. These are computing systems inspired by the human brain's complex network of neurons.

A neural network consists of layers of nodes or 'neurons'. These neurons receive input data, process it, and pass it on to the next layer. The magic of neural networks comes from their ability to learn—to adjust the parameters of this input-processing-output cycle based on the patterns they detect in the data.

Consider a neural network trained to recognize dogs. It starts knowing nothing about what a dog looks like. But, as it's fed thousands of images of dogs, it 'learns' to identify the characteristic patterns—tails, ears, snouts—that define 'dog-ness'. That's neural networks for you: they learn through exposure, much like a child.

2.4. The Power of Deep Learning

Deep learning takes the concept of neural networks and pushes it even further. While a traditional neural network might have one or two layers, deep learning networks, or deep neural networks (DNNs), can have hundreds. Why does depth matter? The answer lies in the kind of patterns DNNs can learn.

In our dog recognizing network, the first few layers might learn to recognize simple shapes like lines and circles. As we go deeper, the network learns to combine these into more complex patterns—eyes, ears, faces. By the time we reach the final layers, the network has learned to recognize 'dog-ness' itself.

This ability to learn hierarchical representations is the secret behind deep learning's success. It's the reason why, from diagnosis prediction in healthcare to autonomous driving in transportation, deep learning is transforming industries across the spectrum.

In conclusion, to understand AI requires us to dig deep into the realms of deep learning and neural networks. It is by grasping these central concepts that we begin to truly comprehend the power, potential, and limitations of AI. This voyage is far from over. In fact, the real adventure is just starting, as we shall explore in the chapters to come, illuminating this extraordinary domain called artificial intelligence.

Prepare yourself for a deep dive into an evolving, exciting world that is pushing boundaries and shaping futures. For we are not just exploring AI from the outside, we are stepping right into the heart of this fascinating digital mind. Together, let's peel back the layers, step by step, and uncover the captivating truth of artificial intelligence.

Chapter 3. Binary Basics: Understanding the Foundation of AI

The discussion of artificial intelligence fundamentally commences with developing the basic understanding of binary concepts. What are binary numbers, and why are they so instrumental to the very foundation of AI?

The word 'binary' stems from bis, a Latin word meaning 'twice'. Effectively, a binary number system is a way of counting that only utilizes two digits, 0 and 1. In simplest terms, these digits are also known as binary digits or 'bits'.

3.1. The Binary Number System

The binary number system, also known as the base-2 number system, is at the heart of all modern computing and digital communications. It's the fundamental language of computers, where data is represented by a series of bits.

Unlike the more familiar decimal number system (which uses ten symbols from 0-9), a binary system uses only two symbols, 0 and 1. Each bit in a binary number represents a power of 2. The rightmost bit represents 2^0, the next represents 2^1, then 2^2, and so forth.

To convert a binary number into decimal form, you simply multiply each bit by a power of 2 and then add the products. For example, the binary number 1101 equals $(1 \times 2^3) + (1 \times 2^2) + (0 \times 2^1) + (1 \times 2^0)$, or 13 in the decimal system.

3.2. The Importance of Binary In Computers

But why do computers use binary, you might ask? Computers operate on electrical signals which exist in one of two states—on or off. Handily, these two states map perfectly to the binary digit values of 0 and 1. Thus, computers represent and manipulate data electronically as binary variables—those that are either on (1) or off (0). Fundamentally, these sequences of 0s and 1s organize themselves into 'strings', and it's the precise arrangements of these strings that form the computer's instructions and data.

Consequently, these binary strings form the essential building blocks of all the higher-level data structures in a computer system. For example, characters such as the letters of the alphabet can be translated into binary numbers using the ASCII system where each character maps to a unique 8-bit binary number.

3.3. Binary Logic

Binary is also used in Boolean logic, the study of truth values through logic gates such as OR, AND, NOT, which form the basis of all computations. With OR and AND acting as basic arithmetic tools, it's easy to build more complex operators like addition, subtraction, multiplication, and division. Each logic gate takes binary inputs, and produces binary outputs based on specific rules.

As an instance, take the AND gate, which requires two binary inputs. If both inputs are 1, the output is 1. For all other combinations, the output is 0. Similarly, the OR gate gives an output of 1 if either or both inputs are 1, and 0 otherwise. The NOT gate has a single input and inverts it—so if the input is 1, it outputs 0, and vice versa. These gates provide the fundamental operation of computers and digital circuits.

3.4. Neural Networks and Binary

When we converge our course towards AI, specifically, neural networks, the importance of binary becomes even more apparant. AI's essence resides in its ability to learn, understand, and emulate human logic.

This is materialized via neural networks, which are inspired by our own biological neural networks. Neural networks represent the mechanics of how our minds learn—creating patterns and making decisions about the world. In these networks, each neuron (or node) corresponds to one 'bit' of information. A node can be 'active' or 'inactive', mirroring the binary concepts of 'on' and 'off' or 1 and 0.

Additionally, the comparison of the input value to a weight (a measure of significance) associated with the node is similar to the AND, OR and NOT logic gate operations. If the product of input and weight exceeds a certain threshold, the neuron is 'activated', otherwise not.

Furthermore, binary codes are also crucial in error detection and correction algorithms, which are paramount to the success of data transmission in AI systems. Parity checks, Hamming codes, and Cyclic Redundancy Checks (CRC) are some examples of error correction mechanisms that fundamentally rely on binary sequences.

To wrap up, Binary is the basic language of computers, the basis of every command, every operation, and also the foundation of implementation and understanding of AI and neural networks. The crux of all computations, whether simple arithmetic or complex machine learning algorithm, are built around this elegant system of zeros and ones. The binary concept, though simple at face value, underpins the magnificent world of computer science and technology, and consequently, AI. Embracing this binary concept is like being handed the magic keys to unlock the fascinating universe of artificial intelligence.

Next time you hear a marvelous tidbit about AI, remember it's all based on the language of binary, spiraling out from the simple 0 and 1 to software able to emulate human intelligence. Indeed, binary might be the most paradigmatic illustration that sometimes, the simplest things underpin the most complex phenomena.

Chapter 4. Neurons and Networks: Mapping the AI Mind

Our journey into the brain of artificial intelligence begins innocuously, with a phenomenon that nature has perfected over millions of years - the neuron. These microscopic entities, the building blocks of human brains, can also be credited directly for the advent of artificial intelligence. However, there's a twist: we're talking about artificial neurons, a concept that forms the foundation of neural networks.

In the early stages of computational technology, scientists and researchers drew inspiration from how the human brain processed information and sought to replicate this astonishing complexity of tasks in machines. From this vision, blossomed the family of algorithms now known as neural networks, with artificial neurons as its key elements.

4.1. Artificial Neurons: Mimicking the Brain

An artificial neuron, just like its biological counterpart, receives inputs, processes them, and generates an output. But instead of dealing with biological signals and chemical synapses, artificial neurons process numerical inputs. This operation is influenced significantly by weights and biases, adjustable elements that determine the significance of each input and the propensity of the neuron to fire, respectively.

Each artificial neuron computes a weighted sum of inputs, adds a bias, and then transforms this value through a non-linear function called an `activation function`. This activation function is the step that introduces a replicative form of neuron firing, where the output is activated only beyond a certain input threshold.

From this high-level view, the concept of an artificial neuron might seem straightforward. But these unique components, when interconnected into networks and unleashed on data, bring forth remarkable abilities.

4.2. Architecture of Neural Networks

The structure of a neural network is heavily borrowed from its namesake, organic neural networks, webs of neurons intricately connected in the brain. This design is known as the `architecture` of the network and typically features layers of interconnected artificial neurons.

A quintessential neural network architecture might include three types of layers:

1. `Input Layer`: This layer receives raw inputs for the network to process. The number of neurons in this layer mirrors the number of features in the dataset.

2. `Hidden Layers`: The layers between input and output layers are called hidden layers. Here, the magical computations and transformations happen. These include activating functions, weights adjustment, and bias optimizations.

3. `Output Layer`: As the name suggests, this layer produces the final output of the neural network. Each artificial neuron in this layer corresponds to a possible predicted category in a classification problem.

Within these layers, imagine countless artificial neurons interacting, their activations pulsing through the network, altering weights and biases in response to error gradients—an orchestra of computation that leads to learning.

4.3. Training Neural Networks: A Cascade of Calculations

Understanding the architecture of neural networks sets the stage for exploring their training methodology. At its core, the training of a neural network revolves around optimizing the weights and biases to reduce error, thus improving predictions. The principal process to achieve this is known as backpropagation.

Backpropagation involves a forward pass and a backward pass:

1. Forward Pass: The network receives an input, processes it layer by layer, and produces an output.

2. Backward Pass: The network calculates the difference between its output and the actual value (known as error or cost), and then spreads the error back through the layers.

During this propagation, the weights and biases are adjusted according to their contribution to the total error, following the principle of Gradient Descent. This optimizes the network's configuration gradually to improve its prediction and reduce the error over time.

However, the path to optimal weights and biases is uphill and replete with mathematical challenges. It's in this uphill journey where fields like calculus, probability, and linear algebra reveal their significance in AI.

4.4. Wrapping up: The Vital Nodes of AI

Artificial neurons are the unsung heroes of the AI revolution. They are not merely mathematical entities but the embodiment of a vision to mimic the incredible computing power of nature in silico. They offer a glimpse into how the simple step of abstracting a biological neuron's operation and replicating it in an artificial format can engineer profound capabilities.

The neural networks are a testament to the power of collective computation. Just like the human brain, where real magic unfolds when billions of neurons work together, the alliance of artificial neurons in multiple layers brings forth the remarkable ability to automatically learn from data.

Delving deeper into neural architecture and training methodologies reveals an arena where multiple domains of mathematics elegantly interweave, fine-tuning the art of predicting and classifying. Artificial neurons, neural networks, and their associated functions form a poetic blend of nature-inspired design, computational wizardry, and mathematical finesse.

Ultimately, it becomes glaringly apparent that neural networks, these vast interconnected webs of artificial neurons processing cascades of computations, are not just software. They are a form of digital darwinism, a microscopic echo of intelligence, and at the very core, a reflection of our scientific curiosity about the mysteries of the brain.

Chapter 5. The Learning Curve: Crash Course on Machine Learning

Machine learning (ML) indeed represents the backbone of artificial intelligence, the key ingredient that empowers computers to learn from direct experience and adapt their responses accordingly, minus explicit programming that predetermines every single decision. Quite similar to a human learner, machines learn. Yet this process bears its unique characteristics, schemas, and protocols.

5.1. Mastering The Basics: What is Machine Learning?

Let's start with an analogy. Imagine you're tossing a ball to your dog. The first few times, the dog might not catch the ball perfectly and won't have the best judgment of how far it needs to go to make that perfect catch. But slowly, with every throw, the dog starts understanding the relationship between the motion of your hand, the movement of the ball, and how much distance it needs to cover. That, in the crudest sense, is learning from experience. Machine learning is the extension of this concept in the world of computers.

Machine learning is a method of data analysis, a type of AI that enables computers to iteratively learn from data, without having to be explicitly programmed to do so. The power to learn automatically and improve from experience is the real game-changer here, allowing machine learning algorithms to find insights hidden within data without even knowing where to look.

The learning can be 'supervised', where the model learns from labeled data [1^], 'unsupervised', where it explores unlabeled data to find patterns [2^], or 'reinforcement' learning, where it learns by a system of reward and penalties in decision-making processes [3^].

[1^] Supervised Learning: The algorithm learns on a labeled dataset, providing an answer key that the algorithm can use to evaluate its accuracy. [2^] Unsupervised Learning: The algorithm explores unlabeled data and finds its own structure within. [3^] Reinforcement Learning: Here the algorithm learns to perform an action from experience.

5.2. Navigating through Types of Machine Learning Algorithms

Now that we've discussed the broad categories of machine learning, let's dive a little deeper into some specific ML algorithms.

5.2.1. Decision Trees

Decision Trees are a type of supervised learning algorithms mostly used for classification problems. A decision tree uses a tree-like model of decisions where each node represents a feature(attribute), each link(branch) represents a decision rule, and each leaf represents an outcome.

5.2.2. Support Vector Machines

A Support Vector Machine (SVM) is another highly effective tool for classification tasks. SVM's primary aim is to create the best line or decision boundary that can segregate n-dimensional space into classes so that we can easily put the new data point in the correct category in the future.

5.2.3. Linear Regression & Logistic Regression

Regression techniques are predictive modeling techniques; linear regression is used for the prediction of continuous outcomes, while logistic regression attempts to predict a categorical outcome.

5.2.4. Neural Networks

Artificial neural networks are biologically inspired networks that extract abstract features from the data in a hierarchical fashion. Neural networks have revolutionized the field of machine learning, giving rise to the era of deep learning and A.I models that can mimic the function of the human brain.

5.3. The Process of Learning: Training a Model

So how really does a machine learn? All these different types of machine learning algorithms mentioned above have one common characteristic: they learn from data. They build a mathematical model based on sample data, known as "training data". This training data helps build a predictive model, and then the performance of the model is gauged based on test data.

The model's performance is assessed based on how well it performed the task and whether the outcome aligns with the label in the test data. Suppose a classification model is being built; in that case, the model's performance might be assessed based on what percentage of instances are correctly classified.

If the model's performance is unsatisfactory, the model is trained again with an adjusted learning algorithm, introducing minor modifications. This process continues until the model performance reaches an acceptable level.

5.4. Machine Learning in Action

Machine Learning is not just a theoretical concept, it is now deeply rooted in the functioning of the real world. From AI personal assistants like Siri and Alexa to recommendation engines of Netflix and Amazon - all are powered by machine learning algorithms.

Other sectors where machine learning has made significant contributions include healthcare and diagnostics, financial trading, pattern and image recognition applications like facial recognition, and many more.

Finally, a wise word about ML. It isn't just a standalone subject; it's a craft that lies at the vivid confluence of mathematics, coding, and problem-solving abilities. Coding allows you to breathe life into those mathematical notions, and good problem-solving skills ensure your model aligns well with the problem at hand.

Machine Learning is perpetual learning, where every setback holds the potential for insights. Through continuous tuning, tweaking, and practicing, we attain mastery over the craft; in turn, introducing the world to new dimensions of innovations and efficiencies.

Step onto this journey of empowering machines with the ability to 'learn'! We guarantee you; it's a journey that's as transformative and insightful as much as the destination! So here's to embracing the unknown, starting from the first code and the first model to the countless that follow!

Chapter 6. Deep Learning Deciphered: Unraveling Complex Concepts

Deep learning, one of the most rapidly evolving fields under the umbrella of AI, often seems complex due to the magnitude of mathematical computations involved and the heavy use of terminology. But fret not, this section will elucidate everything you need to understand about deep learning - its concept, application, transformational power, and future prospects.

Let's kick-start our understanding of deep learning by addressing one fundamental question: What exactly is deep learning?

In layman's terms, deep learning is the branch of AI that emulates the workings of the human brain in processing data for use in decision making. It is a subtype of machine learning with networks capable of learning unsupervised from data that is unstructured. Think of it as an automatic, self-educating system that can enrich its learning over time.

6.1. The Neural Network Relationship

To comprehend deep learning, it's crucial to understand the concept of neural networks. A neural network aims to simulate the activities of the human brain—generating insights or decisions based on the input data. Each neuron within the network processes an element of the input data and passes on the output to the next layer.

Deep learning models are neural networks, but with a twist. A typical neural network contains 2-3 hidden layers while a deep learning algorithm could use thousands. The "deep" in deep learning isn't a reference to any profound enlightenment. It stands for this idea of successive layers of representations.

6.2. Understanding Layered Representations

You might be wondering how these layer-based representations work. Let's make it simpler with a daily-life comparison. Imagine attempting to identify dogs in images. The first layer of the deep learning model will scan for lines or edges, the next layer seeks out the combination of lines or colors that make up shapes or textures, the layer after that identifies patterns like ears and nose specific to dogs. The final layer puts these patterns together and confirms whether the image has a dog or not.

Each successive layer uses the output from the previous one to sharpen its idea of what it's seeing. This process can go on and on until we have a highly accurate model that can recognize complex patterns and objects with minimal error.

6.3. A Dive into Deep Learning Architectures

When it comes to deep learning architectures, there mainly includes deep neural networks, deep belief networks, recurrent neural networks, and convolutional neural networks. These architectures are used for a range of applications such as automatic speech recognition, image and video processing, natural language processing, and even in self-driving cars.

Of all these, Convolutional Neural Networks (CNNs), are one of the most popular architectures in deep learning. CNNs are explicitly designed to recognize grid-like topology data, such as an image that can be interpreted as a grid of pixels. Similarly, Recurrent Neural Networks (RNNs) are popular in natural language processing, considering their ability to remember previous input in the sequence, utilizing the same to influence the current input and output.

6.4. Deep Learning's Computational Intensity

One pivotal aspect of deep learning is its voracious appetite for data and processing power. The 'deep' neural networks demand huge quantities of training data to be able to make precise predictions. Additionally, these models require high computational power and time to learn and generate results.

6.5. Future Developments in Deep Learning

Advancements continue at a strong pace in the field of deep learning. More efficient training methods, novel network architectures, and condensed models for running on less powerful devices are the forefront of this burgeoning field. It continues to be used in most AI undertakings, pushing boundaries across sectors ranging from healthcare to autonomous driving, bringing more autonomy and efficiency into our lives.

There exist numerous concerns about the impact of AI, particularly with the continued expansion of deep learning. However, it's a powerful tool that holds immense potential to drive societal development. With a blend of wise regulation and technical advancement, we can ensure that the world of deep learning continues to benefit humanity, and not become an uncontrolled force.

At its core, deep learning is not as complex as it seems to be. With each layer, computation, and neuron, we are merely replicating the human mind's operation, taking us closer to creating machines that can learn, think, and make informed decisions.

In this fascinating journey through the world of deep learning, you've broken down the boundaries, navigated the complexities, and arrived on the other side with a deeper understanding of the neural networks. Remember, understanding is the first step towards mastery. Your journey into artificial intelligence may seem intricate at times, but as with any subject, its complexities make it that much more interesting to explore and master.

Chapter 7. AI in Action: Real-world Applications of Neural Networks

Artificial Intelligence is on the rise. About a decade ago, AI was a niche technology limited to academics and tech wizards. Today, however, its applications span across industries, seamlessly integrating with our daily lives. Neural networks, a subset of AI, are the driving force behind these advancements. Their ability to learn and adapt creates solutions that were unimaginable a few years back. But the real question is, how exactly does AI, powered by neural networks, manifest in the world around us?

7.1. Everyday Life

When you ask Siri about today's weather, scroll through your personalized Netflix recommendations, or unlock your smartphone using facial recognition—all of these activities are facilitated by neural networks.

Let's take a closer look at facial recognition. This feature boils down to the identification and verification of individuals based on their facial features. A neural network gets trained on millions of images, learning to discern intricate details like the distance between the eyes or the curve of a chin. By comparing these measurements against the saved data, the neural network can determine who's trying to unlock the phone.

Each time you interact with these technologies, you're training the neural network to perform better, enabling it to offer increasingly accurate and personalized results.

7.2. Healthcare

In healthcare, neural networks play a pivotal role. They help with disease diagnostics, drug discovery, patient monitoring, and more. For example, convolutional neural networks (CNNs)—a class of deep learning models—are often used for medical imaging. A CNN can be trained on thousands of radiology images to detect anomalies like tumors or fractures.

These predictions help doctors in fast and accurate diagnosis, thus ensuring the patient gets the right treatment at the right time. However, it's important to note that these models don't replace doctors but augment their capabilities.

7.3. Finance

Neural networks have also found adoption in the financial industry, contributing to fraud detection, algorithmic trading, loan underwriting, and more. These applications leverage the predictive power of neural networks.

For instance, a neural network used for fraud detection is trained on records of fraudulent and non-fraudulent transactions. It learns to flag unusual patterns, such as unexpected high-volume transactions or suspicious behavior indicative of potential fraud.

7.4. Transportation

The transportation sector, and in particular autonomous vehicles, largely benefits from neural networks. Technologies like Tesla Autopilot use a type of neural network called Long Short-Term Memory (LSTM) to predict road conditions, detect obstructions, and effectively navigate using in-built sensors and cameras.

7.5. Cybersecurity

In the cybersecurity domain, neural networks are efficient sentinels. They process vast amounts of data to identify anomalies in networks, such as unauthorized access or unusual data transfers, signaling potential cyber threats.

7.6. Climate Modelling

In environmental science, neural networks assist in assessing climate change, predicting weather patterns, and modeling complex ecological systems. Such implementations often use multi-layered feed-forward networks that learn extremely large and complex datasets.

From describing present patterns to predicting future trends, these tools offer an unparalleled ability to understand and combat climate change impacts.

7.7. Manufacturing

Neural networks in manufacturing provide predictive maintenance, product quality verification, supply chain optimization, among other applications. Using historical data, a neural network can predict when a machine is likely to fail, thereby saving resources and avoiding unexpected downtime.

7.8. Conclusion

This broad overview does not capture all applications of neural networks, as new uses continue to be developed across industries globally. As our understanding and ability to implement these networks deepen, so does the scope of their application. It is no understatement that we are in the midst of an AI revolution, and neural networks stand at its core, poised to redefine our world in ways that we can only begin to imagine.

Remember, AI and neural networks aren't something that's coming—they're here, and you interact with them every day. The increased adoption and proliferation of this technology promise more personalized services, efficient solutions, and ultimately, an improved quality of life for everyone.

Chapter 8. The Great AI Debate: Ethics, Implications and Discussions

As countless science fiction tales suggest, artificial intelligence carries with it potential for both utopia and dystopia. The imagined future swings from humanity dwelling in a bliss of AI-assisted comfort, to a cinematic nightmare where machines stand in control. As we stand on the precipice of tomorrow, it is urgent to navigate the dueling narratives surrounding AI, scrutinizing not just its capabilities, but its moral and ethical implications.

8.1. The Duality of AI: Benefaction or Catastrophe

On one flank, AI holds limitless promises. AI systems drive time-saving automations, pave roads towards medical breakthroughs, inspire novel avenues for exploration in artificial creativity and offer unprecedented tools for data analyses. Simultaneously, the advent of this technology raises specters from the depths of our collective imagination: loss of jobs due to automation, rampant surveillance states, deep fake misuse, the specter of autonomous weapons, and even fears of a 'Singularity'—an imagined future where AI surpasses human intelligence, potentially to our doom.

8.2. Ethics of AI Development

Casting the dire predictions aside, ethical contemplations need immediate addressing. Algorithms, essentially a reflection of programmer biases, can unintentionally establish patterns of discrimination and inequality in their predictions. Is it fair, for example, for an AI system to establish hiring decisions, potentially weaving subtle biases into the choosing process?

Equally pressing is the question of explaining AI decisions. Known as the 'black box' problem, it can be incredibly challenging, often impossible, to understand how complex AI systems arrive at their decisions. If an AI system misjudges, assigns blame or neglects an entity, who becomes responsible? Is it the developers, the implementers, the users, or the AI itself? And how does society go about serving justice?

8.3. AI and Automation: The Job Market's Friend or Foe?

Advancements in artificial intelligence, machine learning, and robotics have triggered renewed fear of job loss due to automation. As industrial machines replaced laborers in the first and second industrial revolutions, nuances reside in predicting the consequences of AI-driven fourth industrial revolution. Certainly, the rise of AI will displace some jobs, but it will also create others, just as steam power, electricity, and the assembly line did in their time. A crucial challenge, among others, is ensuring smooth transitions and achieving fair distributions of the benefits.

8.4. AI and Privacy: A Delicate Balance

The development and scaling of AI systems invariably coincide with robust data collection. Not only does this mass surveillance culture fuel the privacy debate, but it also touches on democratic and authoritarian approaches in using AI. How can societies harness the potentials of AI while respecting the individual's right to privacy? And in light of possible misuse such as deepfakes or misinformation campaigns, how do we balance the open-source ethos of AI research?

8.5. Defense AI: Pros and Cons

The utilization of AI in military operations opens yet another ethical dilemma. While AI-integrated systems promise to reduce casualties by executing dangerous tasks, the notion of 'killer robots'—autonomous weapons that decide targets without human intervention—is nothing short of horrifying. It brings forth a debate raging on in international forums: should there be a preemptive ban on lethal autonomous weapons?

8.6. The Ghost of Singularity

While it forms the pinnacle of sci-fi speculation, the concept of Singularity, a stage where AI surpasses human intelligence and self-improves at an exponential rate, entails grave potential consequences. Would such a superintelligent entity uphold the best interest of humanity, assuming it would even be capable of such a consideration? Who decides what this 'best interest' is and how to achieve it? Scholars argue for safeguards and controlled development to avert any ill-devised sci-fi endings.

In conclusion, the ethical and societal implications of AI outstretch beyond simple good-versus-evil or utopia-versus-dystopia narratives. As we stand at a transformative moment in human history, the development and deployment of AI systems demand careful scrutiny and precaution. The great AI debate explores not just the innovations, but the humanistic, ethical, and moral dimensions inherent in the proliferation of artificial intelligence. With skilful navigation, we may surf the wave of AI revolution to better shores, sidestepping the turbulence. On a smaller scale, handling AI with ethics in mind aligns the technology's intention with ours, thereby carving a harmonious shared existence.

Chapter 9. AI in the Future: Predictions and Possibilities

As we navigate the landscape of AI, understanding its current state brings thought-provoking contemplation about the future. To all those who experience awe when first exposed to AI and its stellar capabilities, we promise an exhilarating journey of theorizing potential transitions and outcomes.

9.1. Predictions: Envisaging the Future of AI

In predicting AI's future, it is paramount to consider multiple sources: academic, commercial, and government. These often harbor different objectives and hence varying perspectives on AI's trajectory.

While AI has come a long way from its nascent stages, riding on technological advancements and computing power, the landscape is set to become even more fascinating. Advancements in algorithms, data collection, machine learning, and neural networks propose an evolutionary shift towards more robust and comprehensive AI capabilities. Here are some educated predictions on where AI may lead us next:

- Strong AI: Today, we are accompanied by narrow (or weak) AI, systems designed to perform specific tasks, like voice recognition or internet searches. The future, however, could bloom with strong AI: systems that aren't restricted to single, specialized tasks, but instead exhibit human levels of understanding and reasoning. Progress may be time-consuming and fraught with challenges, but the advent of strong AI could redefine society and human interaction.

- Improved Decision Making: Machine learning algorithms and neural networks are rapidly being integrated into systems to aid decision-making. Expect these mechanisms to become more accurate, auto-corrective, and adaptive, resulting in more efficient services across industries.

- Autonomous Systems: Global industries, from manufacturing to transportation, might soon harbor fully autonomous systems. With AI advancing towards sophisticated understanding and decision-making, and with increased IoT integration, such systems could soon be commonplace.

- Morality-infused AI: As AI integrates increasingly into societal frameworks, the demand for ethical considerations in AI systems will rise. This could potentially lead to the development of AI that is mindful of ethical and societal norms, blurring the line between humane and artificial betterment.

9.2. Possibilities: Unleashed Potential of AI

Looking even further ahead, AI's prospects broaden when we factor in radical technology innovations. Pioneers in AI research and development are already exploring these realms. Get ready to feast your imagination on an awe-inspiring spectrum of possibilities:

- Immortality through AI: Science fiction often imagines digital consciousness transfer as a form of immortality. We may still be far from such a reality, but advancements in neural networks and data preservation techniques have sparked dialogue around consciousness emulation in AI systems.

- Superintelligence: This term represents AI surpassing human intelligence in virtually every possible aspect, ranging from creative pursuits to scientific understanding. While controversial and clouded by uncertainties, its eventual manifestation cannot be discarded from the gamut of possibilities.

- AI-Human Symbiosis: Instead of contemplating AI as an external entity, embedding AI within the human body, enhancing physical and cognitive abilities, might be the future. Scientists are probing into bio-compatible AI, potentially converging biological life with digital intelligence.

9.3. Obstacles: The Challenges in Making Predictions a Reality

Predicting the future of tech as vast and intricate as AI comes with its own set of hurdles. These are some prominent challenges that AI might face in its progression.

- Ethical Quandary: As AI increasingly filters into society, ethical implications could pose significant roadblocks. Addressing the issue would involve complex political, moral, and philosophical debates, alongside technological advancements.

- AI Control Problem: If we ever develop superintelligent AI, a pertinent question arises: How can we ensure it will act in humanity's best interests?

- Legal Considerations: AI's integration into several facets of life might result in a legal framework reform, especially concerning responsibility and accountability.

- Technical Constraints: Conceptual and practical challenges might slow AI's evolution towards strong AI and superintelligence. Our current understanding of such systems remains minimal, demanding exceptional breakthroughs for significant progress.

9.4. The Path Ahead

The anticipation surrounding AI's potential evolution stirs excitement, curiosity, and fear, all at once. Though rooted in conjecture, the prospects we discussed are within the realms of possibility. Enshrining AI's future with ethics, sustainability, and human benefit at its core would ensure not just technological progression, but societal evolution. In this endeavor, humanity's collective wisdom will play a crucial role.

The future of AI is a canvas spread before us; it's a narrative waiting to be penned. It invites us to debate, to speculate, to fear, and to hope. AI's journey into the future promises much more than advancement—it promises the opportunity to shape an epoch-defining technology, to ensure that it serves humanity and not replaces it. We, at the helm, have the remarkable privilege to steer this transformative force, and therein lies our tremendous responsibility.

Through understanding and insight, we equip ourselves to face this evolving horizon. We strive to retain human values whilst adapting to alterations in the terrain. As we stand on the precipice of unimaginable transformations, let's look towards the AI-centric future with preparedness and optimism, and remember, the power to guide this revolution resides with us.

Chapter 10. The AI Toolbox: Resources for Further Learning

In this era of amplified technological advancements, artificial intelligence has placed itself as an imperative sector, a toolbox if you will, possessing the potential to revolutionize nearly every facet of our lives. And within this toolbox, we find a variety of tools designed not just for implementation, but also for learning and growth. Whether you are taking a first step into this novel realm or seeking to expand your knowledge, we introduce you to an array of useful resources. Each resource, like a unique cog in a larger mechanism, plays a fundamental role in helping you fathom the depth and breadth of AI.

10.1. Books to Start Your AI Journey

For a more detailed, comprehensive understanding of the vast field of AI, books often offer a deep dive into the subject, highlighting key concepts, illustrating examples, and providing an overall cohesive view of this cutting-edge technology. Here are a few recommended titles to anchor your AI journey:

- 'Artificial Intelligence: A Modern Approach' by Stuart Russell and Peter Norvig: Often referred to as the 'AI Bible', this book remains a classic among AI enthusiasts, with its thorough conceptual coverage and illustrated examples.

- 'Hands-On Machine Learning with Scikit-Learn, Keras, and TensorFlow' by Aurélien Geron: If you prefer a hands-on approach, this book is an exceptional guide. It offers practical advice on implementing machine learning models using popular libraries and frameworks.

- 'Deep Learning' by Ian Goodfellow, Yoshua Bengio, and Aaron Courville: Known as the 'Deep Learning Bible', this book offers a deep dive into the topics of machine learning and neural networks - the cornerstone of today's AI technologies.

10.2. Online Courses to Kickstart Your Learning

With digitalization at its zenith, online education platforms have emerged as a significant source of knowledge. These platforms, while providing extensive content, allow you to learn at your own pace. Here are a few online platforms and courses to consider:

- 'Machine Learning' by Andrew Ng on Coursera: This course is often hailed as a perfect starting point for anyone attempting to understand the nuances of machine learning.

- 'Deep Learning Specialization' by Andrew Ng on Coursera: This is a sequence of five courses that delve into neural networks, machine learning's most utilized architecture.

- EdX's 'Professional Certificate in AI': Offered by Columbia University, this program provides a comprehensive understanding of the principles and practices of AI.

10.3. Research Papers and Journals - The Current Frontier

To keep abreast with the AI world's constant evolution, it's crucial to get acquainted with the latest research and advancements. Use the following resources as stepping-stones towards this path:

- 'arXiv.org': A repository of over a million scholarly articles from varied fields, including AI and machine learning, arXiv is an excellent resource to access the most recent research papers.

- 'Journal of Artificial Intelligence Research (JAIR)': This journal offers high-quality, peer-reviewed research papers spanning a broad spectrum of topics in AI.

10.4. Interactive Platforms and Communities

Engaging with AI communities can aid your understanding by providing different perspectives and hands-on solutions to common issues. Several communities also offer interactive platforms where you can experiment with applying AI concepts:

- 'Kaggle': A platform that provides data science competitions, Kaggle lets you apply what you've learned on real-world data, with an engaging community.

- 'GitHub': This is not just a repository for source code; it has an active community where AI enthusiasts share their projects, theories, and ideas.

- 'Reddit (subreddits like /r/MachineLearning, /r/artificial)': These online forums can often offer insights and spark discussions unavailable in traditional educational resources.

10.5. AI Podcasts and Blogs - Learn on the Go

If you're all about multitasking and learning on the go, podcasts and blogs can serve you well in understanding the current trends in AI:

- 'The AI Alignment Podcast': This podcast, hosted by Lucas Perry, explores how humanity can proactively guide AI's impact on society.

- 'Towards Data Science': An online blog that offers insightful articles from various AI practitioners, sharing their experiences and knowledge.

The vastness of AI can be daunting to navigate, but each of the resources mentioned plays a pivotal role in enhancing your understanding and skills. Remember, the journey into AI is not a sprint but a marathon. Take one step at a time. Happy learning!

Chapter 11. Demystifying the A in AI: A Synthesis and Paths Ahead

If there's one invention that has sparked intrigue and dread in equal measure, it is Artificial Intelligence (AI). All pervasive, mysterious, and rife with endless possibilities, AI continues to steer humankind into uncharted territories of innovation, inching us closer every day to a future once imagined solely within the pages of science fiction.

AI, in the simplest of terms, is a form of machine intelligence where an artificial entity (like a computer system) is capable of autonomously making decisions, interpreting data, learning from its experiences, and even predicting future trends. However, is there more to AI than what meets the eye? Let's deep dive to rescue AI from the confounding haze of myths and misconceptions, breaking down its workings, and envisioning a roadmap for its future.

11.1. The Core Elements of AI

The framework of AI, grounded in the realm of computer science, is as complex as it is fascinating, resting upon three pillars: machine learning, deep learning, and neural networks.

Machine Learning (ML) serves as the foundational building block of AI, engendering its ability to learn from data autonomously. ML employs a myriad of algorithms to identify patterns within variable datasets, a self-learning process which, over time, enables AI to make predictions or decisions without being explicitly programmed.

Deep learning, a subset of machine learning, takes this concept a step further. It utilizes artificial neural networks, inspired by the functioning of the human brain. Within these networks, multiple layers of nodes process and transmit data, with each successive layer refining the interpretation of data from the previous one.

The profound parallels between human cognition and machine cognition don't end here. AI's neural networks are also capable of adapting to change. Just like human brains rewire neural pathways based on new experiences or information, AI's neural networks utilize backpropagation for the rectification and advancement of their learning process. This attribute amplifies AI's potential exponentially, manifesting its capability to handle complex and dynamic data sets, evolving its learning beyond static algorithms.

11.2. Apprehending the 'A' in AI

From enabling speech recognition in our smartphones to predicting consumer behavior on e-commerce websites, it's evident that AI's presence is ubiquitous. However, the true nature of the 'A', or the artificiality in AI, often remains enshrouded in mystery.

At its core, the 'artificiality' of AI refers to its non-biological origin and the essence of its manufactured intelligence as opposed to natural, human intelligence. The sophistication of this artificiality varies across AI models, from narrow AI systems that specialize in singular tasks, like voice assistant technologies, to ambitious endeavours towards creating Artificial General Intelligence (AGI), a hypothetical model wherein AI surpasses humans in most economically valuable work.

Perhaps, the most critical aspect of this 'artificiality' is the logic-driven, data-dependent nature of AI, distinctively different from the emotion-influenced, sporadically irrational human mind. This contrast often fuels concerns about AI's potential overreach, its impacts on privacy, employment, and ultimately, humanity's future as a whole.

11.3. Decoding AI's Potentials and Pitfalls

As a subject of heated debates, AI is often saluted for its achievements while simultaneously feared for its potential risks. Recognizing this divide is essential for responsibly leveraging AI.

On the beneficial front, AI powered innovations such as automation technologies have revolutionized industries, from healthcare with its AI-supported diagnostic tools, to agriculture where AI-backed machinery is enhancing crop yields. AI's miraculous feats also extend to defeating humans in complex games like Chess and Go, demonstrating its analytical prowess.

However, AI also harbors its fair share of challenges. A primary concern is the labor force's displacement thanks to automation. Further, AI systems have a tendency to act as 'black boxes', with their decision-making processes often remaining opaque. Unbridled reliance on AI without understanding how a decision was made could lead to ethical and moral dilemmas.

An infamous example is the facial recognition technology. While serving as an effective security measure, it has fallen under scrutiny for racial bias within its algorithms, reinforcing the urgency for ethical regulations around AI's use.

11.4. Plotting the Future: Paths Ahead

As AI straddles between promise and peril, foreseeing its future necessitates a balanced approach. A possible roadmap embraces four avenues:

1. **Capitalization on Opportunities**: Continue harnessing AI for

process efficiency, improved decision-making, and driving innovation across sectors.

2. **Promotion of AI Literacy**: Foster widespread awareness and understanding about AI, dispelling myths and fueling informed discussions.

3. **Prioritizing Cybersecurity**: As AI systems become more prevalent, they become likely targets for cyberattacks. Prioritizing robust, impenetrable systems is non-negotiable.

4. **Strong Regulations and Ethical Guidelines**: Implementing standardized protocols and ethical guidelines can mitigate unintended consequences while ensuring fair and responsible use of AI.

AI, with its intricate labyrinth of capabilities and potential risks, encapsulates the pinnacle of technological revolution. As we continue to demystify AI, we must tread consciously, maintaining a fine balance between leveraging its benefits and mitigating its threats. Unraveling the 'A' in AI is just scratching the surface, the depths of AI remain waiting to be explored. Will we allow fear to hold us back, or can we step forth boldly into this brave new world? Only time will tell.